The Sleep That Changed Everything

WESLEYAN POETRY

LEE ANN BROWN

The Sleep
That Changed Everything

WESLEYAN UNIVERSITY PRESS
MIDDLETOWN, CONNECTICUT

Published by Wesleyan University Press,
Middletown, CT 05459

©2003 by Lee Ann Brown
Designed by Dean Bornstein

Printed in the United States of America 5 4 3 2 1

Library of Congress Cataloging-in-Publication Data

Brown, Lee Ann.
  The sleep that changed everything / Lee Ann Brown.
    p. cm. — (Wesleyan poetry)
  ISBN 0–8195–6621–7 (alk. paper) — ISBN 0–8195–6622–5
    (pbk.: alk. paper)
  I. Title. II. Series.
  PS3552.R6932S57 2003
  811'.6 — dc21   2002155482

To
You

the Other

to
Poets
to
Come

and to

Stephanie Jane Harrison (1964–1986)
Harry Smith (1923–1991)
Marjorie Keller (1951–1994)
Joe Brainard (1942–1994)
Hannah Weiner (1928–1997)
Allen Ginsberg (1926–1997)

Agnes Lee Dunlop Wiley
my maternal grandmother
(New Year's Eve, 1902–Valentine's Day, 1999)

CONTENTS

INFLORESENCE

In Infloresence

❦ x ❧

ACKNOWLEDGMENTS

Versions of these poems have appeared
in the following publications:

The Baffler, Booglit Boogmark, The Capilano Review, Chain,
Combo, Crow, Downtown Brooklyn, Explosive, Fence, The Hat,
How2, Insurance, Jacket, No Trees, Oasis Broadside, Pressed Wafer,
Primary Writing, Proteus, Skanky Possom, Snare, Verse
and in
How2 Write Love Poems that Don't Suck
by dELiA's & Charles Weigl;
Miss Traduction:
Homophonic Translations from the American, Dutch,
French and Latin (Tender Buttons, 1995);
Reverse Mermaid / The Thirteenth Sunday in Ordinary Time
(Belladonna, 2001);
and
The Voluptuary Lion Poems of Spring (Tender Buttons, 1997).

In these Anthologies:
An Anthology of International Avant-garde Poetry in English,
edited by Rod Menghem & John Kinsella (Salt);
An Anthology of New (American) Poets,
editors: Lisa Jarnot, Chris Stroffolino and Leonard Schwartz;
The Best American Poetry 2001, edited by Robert Hass;
Blood & Tears: Poems for Matthew Shepard edited by Scott Gibson;
and
The Portable Boog Reader, edited by David Kirschenbaum.

Thank you to all the editors who have encouraged my work,
and to the curators of readings where these poems first aired.

The author would also like to thank
Djerassi Artists' Residency,
Foundation Royaumont,
Rocky Mountain Women's Institute,
Virginia Center for the Creative Arts,
Yaddo
and
the Fund for Poetry
for time and support to work on this book.

INSUFFLATION

an act of blowing on, into, or in

❧ ❧ ❧

a Christian ceremonial rite of exorcism performed
by breathing on a person

❧ ❧ ❧

the act of blowing something (as a gas, powder, or vapor)
into a body cavity

It remains   (Alice Notley)
read poetry
and imagine yourself writing it

A poet is a mirror, a transcriber   (Susan Howe)

❦ 2 ❧

What are these wingèd words

(Jennifer Moxley)

Creating community around poetry
(typically NYS)

Other peoples' vocabularies did this to me.

Auspicious Window

Between sky & town
Birds sing   Bells ring
Venus ascends   the Starry Stair
While afternoon comes upon
Our fair histories

Sensitive plants touch but
Stay open past twilight.
Between rearranged lines
Walking, lives a moth.
A flaming sigh
Takes us   past our
pain   almost
Human   Lucky
A brief   Communication
Fortuitous   Window never
Written,   go on

A Call for Vertical Integration in the Eye of the Storm

Purple & blue Tiffany combo in the
Church of my childhood struggle of perfect
Public meat longing again vine-covered
Power flower conflict hunger for green

Struggle—if this is sin then separation—
Grace abounds even more than bonds—
Doubt boundaries not programmable—
Stretched grace strikes us down—
Social eels demand ransom, children

Do not bow your heads—tranquility of hymns
Is shattered & addressed two days ago I
Saw the Black Ash of a Church Burned on its
Sure Foundation   Century old pin oaks scorched

Against stones of those who can't ever leave this sight—
Who witnessed   Who
Drove away during the sermon   Burning

Cometary

Come lay here awhile familiar body of earth
swelling sweetness I know not yet

When sexing grows stale so will living so
not yet to die or be bored by bright
eyes in the bias of night streaming
3 am comfortable garlic   rose
honey   jasper   beryllium   iridium
insulating who knows what from whom or
what marginalia starts to cook at
3 pm half way cross to one real world
writing flash across the sky complete
with fiery tail   Just once is not
enough how 'bout 4 a minute
and look up again tonight

Come here   Come tarry

Comet her

Encyclopedia Botanica

or

A Mother-to-Be's Book of meltdown anticipation and scientific renderings of organic and theoretical forms such as the way flowers lie in the bud: A permutational Cento of Centos consisting of painful insufflations, multiple estivations, the calculus of various inflorescents, my naive set theories (as unordered pairs), vibratory odes in all manner of cross-pollinating color, illumined spores & how they grow in corkscrew contortion, all imbued with entire New Electric Libraries of the Body. Herein find random factors of the strange attraction to "hard science," but also to soften it, previously FAILED materials and pick-up works, illuminated maps of misreading, specifically, a Trace Study of my Own Peculiar Vocabulary living in the dictionary, reading public signs backwards or torqued in the House (See: "Waking in the Offices of Dawn," "A Demand for Fried Chicken," and "The Unhinged Bride's Index Box"). A deep pillow tapestry, the soft underbelly of the (not guilty) quilt-lined snow on 100's of 1000's of flowers packed in wet newspaper to last this linked act always with an Other in mind: molecules being excited to a higher level of activity by heat or unseen stimulations, through any reader's eye to correspondence's finger, culminating in a Splice Index for the edification of Ladies, Gentlemen, Sentences & new Punkish Geezers left out in the rain of the Sleep Cake that changed Everything.

Insufflation

for Tom Raworth

Fresh start
she smokes
the color of his eyes
rat, maternal & sexual behavior

in that culture
there was husband capture
the word for inhaling someone else

"stay" plain
an insufflating venture
inventing all the ways of from

as for me and mine
we know how water changes
pitch as it warms up &
connects the poem's skin up to
curvaceous thought
& open possibles,
pricks up the spring like
songs

my liner notes are
nonlinear notes

Linear Velocity
in a Velocity line

Children meeting
you can only try

Not to subsume
the title into the poem

Words like "crank" & "shift"
"frame"
Thinking as
sexually inspired not so
far from the idea of what
makes me write

Vibratory Ode
Not to work my Vibratory Mode
was one option
I close to forego

What happened to me?
I tried to be like everybody
else for a few moments
out the window

Insufflation
loss or relation or
In your face
elation
suffered inflation
Play it in its
identification

I feel like I can't read
people's poems
without loving them
Just having met he said
Tell me everything right now
& give it to me right now on stone
· tablets right now please

My other story:
Upon trying to find some Barbecue
in Greensboro, NC on a Sunday night
& upon the suggestion of
a restaurant named I forget what,
She said, "No, that's Black Tie"
& I thought she meant
"Pigfoot with Lemongrass"

I can tell Electricity

I've often been too literal & try
Always to fly over the wings

    And what does a body do without its desires?
    It tries to get them back   (Carla Harryman)

I'm your irreversible Holiday Guest
The phone rang as we walked in the door
Sorry we missed each other
any exchange of info

or Phraseology

I limit my register
Relegation   Regulation
Regulating
the specifics of her
encircling the rhythmic phrase
Embrace loneliness & get over it

"What's normal to you
is strange to me"

Muscle in on
Collage as a grid
I am read
What would you like
(Morningfade)
Too late to lay straight out
Music spins too short to cut back
Amazingly unformulaic exchange of modes
No memory any more than
writing without remembering

Mural pout   icy blue irises   taste salty
Negative lotion or prosthetic nerve
Too beautiful for use
Exclusive of description
Distant radio blur   pensive not
some kind of horrible rhythm
Grinning mask
The black church vibrates
That's not nice

I'll tell you a story
Meager income not sleep
Driver to tense up the flowers
Fetch the muscular job
Lack thereof when indifference flutters
Not impressed by personality
Scratch "Music"
Hanging up the phone
Any trick to sit still
Dependent on time not motor vehicles
In the mode of
grabbing the meat
Money exchanged hands

Laying the book flat
She worked it out
The sunlight offered solution

Calling in sick
the ceiling crumbles
Stages of dreaming
travel & funeral
Forgetting the text
Deserted not waiting
a titular running away
Writing for the "ing"
Every click startles my little girl
A father I wish I never had
Back sliding emotion
Curious about devolution
Too busy or not so (with the dailies)
Balance sheets tear my eye
A star staring
Forcing myself on myself
Auto treble singes the cut
Extra "E" why kill a moth?
Harsh detail driven in with a nail
Phraseology stiffens and pumps
Missing its next opportunity
Working together for a moment
As if compatibility were a muscle
Too much resistance
Preponderance too normal
Spoiled bourgeosie me
What could they have but beauty
Backwards medal a moment
nerve out still proceeding
stacatto endurance

tongue tied missive never arrived
or even called
never picked up
as in the machine hung up
not like I imagined
a cricket under the fridge
plate goes back to sleep
"spot" as percussive
derivative protest
byzantine frustration
under any circumstance
either deal or freak
momentum taboos the corner store
Easter morning alone
Setting myself up to be toughened
a spectrum of hair
Unanthologized Beat
spun out into
reading it sometimes to myself
see if I can still
end up waiting no matter what
might as well find a way to work
Need a scar   a notice stressed
Struck through quotation marks

Poet's Complaint

Exercising the drill bit in my mouth
I am past working for the man
Yet must do it again—
Again do it must I
Like every poor sod
Guiltily sapping on lazy-nesses
Bed of down right Southern
Insolence—Mules & Drugs
Sleepy of culture
Culture of sleepy
Walking in pumps sumped
Out to yards of S. O'Hara's spoiler.
Miss Scarlet Mars on Venus moons:
O Muser be my Abuser!
Wake up—Atalanta's burning!
When will I again be evicted
From this Divine Sepulchre?
When will I get my jump
Astarted from above?
Athena should be leaner
Brand me again
With the mark of the Breast!
I need a Wing Haven
I need a Thrush Band
Of gypsies holding
Mirrors to my waste.
I need a Lark who sings
So out of tune so as to
Shake me to my roots—
But please can you make it not hurt
So much

Like last time?
Pull my hair only hard enough
To make it
Grow greener than grass
& Death seem so near
But not yet here

Respond to me

Respond to me: how many
iniquities have I and fish. Scholar me
& delicate easterns to me.

Simple curs abscond with you
& are arbitrarily inimicable to you?

Against leaves, what raptors I buy

East and potentates to aim
and stipendly sic'em on persecutors:

Writers & enemies against my sailor lovers
consume me, consume my fish
my many sad scents

Positronic in my nervous pedestals
& observing all vastness
my many cementings
& my vestigial feet meow considerately:

How quasi I redo considerable sums, how
invested, how comedic a tin ear.

shiny jewel eye

with Julie Patton, Euphrosyne Bloom & Meg Arthurs in mind

These flower forms vary to me in ways I can't say yet but you
know already before me in your dress lace—no "A" on the off
white (cream) lady bugged familiar to the wall pointing to Big
Ohio Egyptian football in & out motion of your arms passion
freak—out on our own time—to the triumphs flower—the stole
slipped, the slip stole—no limits on the feintly fealty couch—
passive as he was—(I'm huge)—the hinge bing-cherried out
& tweaked on the Byronic road ironic—drownded in the lake
of Prague's Guarda—Valve without me—he's—free—and
Sphinx-like as I write the night again so quick—The Dion Ferry
is X-otic—water taxied over Manhatta's spires

where (back in time) she was living in Alphabet City with all the
little stories she never tells:

While throwing an apple peel over her shoulder she suddenly re-
alizes she's been living in Description City all along. A big, blue
letter "A" is motioning for her over to take off her veil and play,
but she says 'fuck that' while chewing on her candy cigarettes.
The Phantom Tollbooths, otherwise known as the Fuss Puppets,
are now warming up in the room covered entirely with writing.
One says "Dogmatic No Radio" and another, just "Spike."

Ms. (Blank) was trying to think but it was real hard because of
all the buzzing. People kept trying to get her attention and suc-
ceeding. She had started to live alone once, but like honey he
started living there too, postponing her growing up for a few
more months.

She lived in the zone whose even years no solstice interrupt.
A certain surgeon had a beautiful garden there. He stuttered
even further when trying to speak his own name. There remains

a small scar on her forefinger where she cut herself in the university kitchens. Blood ran all down her apron as she inadvertently hoisted the large carrot, repairing back to her room. A Russian Formalist toy made of colored wood was waiting there.

She converted to Sarah Beattyism, then more slowly to Quietism. *Single Girl, Single Girl, Goes where she please. Married Girl, Married Girl: Baby on her knees Baby on her knees.* If one more guy tells me they like that song, I'm going to Crown Him (in not a nice way).

Hot nights in the summer bedroom astrological Grand Central Station. Fox Point Kitchen Dance. Mingus was a Big Band trying to affect my body with some immediate gravity. Sex do to me one's catalogue and while you're at it Rimbaud. The cats had better but fewer houses. Let all mortal flesh keep silent over that one. The seraphim with ceaseless eye knew their metempsychosis was incomplete.

So formally, she was nowhere yet. But the dream takes its own form, organically arranged like a bento box, that is, organic within the waking grid.

Whitman Poem   "Come . . ."

See the many blossoms of the field:
      Each blade shines with an infinity of flowers,
          each blowing its life away—
              Pollen carried in the wind, Sing!

To the wind, Clover, wild rose, sturdy Mullen,
      purple Larch and Dog violet, twiny Jute,
          tiny Pipsissiwa all connected underground,
              Pokeweed's vivid juice on my skin:

To all the plants, flowering weeds and grasses:
      Cinquefoil, Wild Columbine, Rue, Bergamot:

All Gorgeous Companions,

Let's lay our warm bodies down on the warmer earth.

Let me lay my head on your chest and feel your breath . . .

All around us the grasses are blooming as we are,
entering and mixing, one into another!

ESTIVATION

The way flower petals lie in the bud

or

to pass the summer in a state of torpor—compare HIBERNATION

Faces and forms, I would write
        you down
In a style of leaves growing.

(Louis Zukofsky)

❦ 20 ❧

Unseen buds, infinite, hidden well,
Under the snow and ice, under the darkness, in every square or
cubic inch,

Like babes in wombs, latent, folded, compact, sleeping

(Walt Whitman)

I want   certain

words

more than a thousand flowers

(Cibo Matto)

Convolute

all our hypertridimensional lives

Involute

Curling heart
You're all wrought up
But any to open
at ready given moment

A byzantine course description

A wild menu   moves the feast to violet

                      blue

                         milky

We must curl in reverse
We must curl in cruelty
We must eat

                 (Lyn Hejinian)

O my little Contradiction what terms
like Cover and Sleeper

can't rejoin broad daylight over
a former part of life
now seen as mystery data via the
departmental arts
I mean to vie for
Being a Sleeper

The idea cringes to be called that.
What if paper were longer?
Wincing, he winges, so winged.

An involute trip through
in search of your own part

Forms of unfinished estivation
Flip in as in Neuromancer

   the floral clock

   sidereal

   Available light
or light while there *is* light

Why privilege any one
bead of the necklace
or borrow a boring music?

  50 curls
   then

The sidewalks of Winesburg, Ohio
roll up in a spiral
having been wound so closely around their axis

His Insulators are of the varigated lingerie variety
We bake screw muffins in the sun

Everything seems real decadent as the decade rolls up

In botany flowers continue to bloom
In the country, same thing

In geometry a curve is traced by the end of a taut string
    when it is wound upon or unwound from a fixed curve
    on the same plane with it
    like the bright green bean vines wildly crawling up

An involving or being involved (entanglement or complication)

As when he said I had
"Byzantine ideas of human sexual relationships."

I had to look it up when he left the room.

    O you involute poets, yelping and mating
    with your own kind on the rocky crags:

    Don't do the Poetry Slam!

    Turning in on one's self.

    Think I'll turn in now.

    Turn into what?

Obvolute

Two lips link
in overlapping margins

Quincunx

Sucking on Mary's Spoon

I was

Cat mound rests her place

What will happen next

a pregnant curl of a bloom

not new but

referencing other flowers

Anthos legere

flowers & brambles

a tangled swamp

fall leaves rain

fall   leaves   fall

Revolute

Turning towards you

Something's gotta give

viridian green pleads her case

The sickbook is full today—

Come back tomorrow

feathery stitches + + +

                                             pure joy

feather y   stitches   / / /   unfinished estivation

the bud unfurl   ed
   like my fin ger s
in a fi st
            of pi nk not
            thr eatening to you r

oblivi on

Rose Clothed Ahead

for Coby Batty & his wolf-dog Hazel

peacocks in the rafters

written in blue vectors

in the vortex red

working in concert

in this our

sad & beautiful world

outside the video

brimming with memories

the rain comes again

steady in your mouth

the peace lily blooms

we reach people

in waves

be careful

It's porn out there

pokeberries where

In my mind

peacocks in the sheet mettle

Welcome to the

secular sexular

church of happiness

Succubi & Incubi

altogether now

peruse and pursue

your spider music

The good life fell out

of your book

so I put it back

in the middle

of grace

in the greys

she diffused it

a 'peace genius'

walking down the middle

VIBRATORY
ODES

*a periodic motion of the particles of an elastic body or medium
in alternately opposite directions from the position of equilibrium
when that equilibrium has been disturbed (as when a stretched
cord produces musical tones or particles of air transmit
sounds to the ear)*

✦✦✦

a quivering or trembling motion

✦✦✦

*a characteristic emanation, aura, or spirit that infuses or
vitalizes someone or something that can be instinctively sensed
or experienced—often used in plural, a distinctive usually
emotional atmosphere capable of being sensed*

My little butterfly butters my bread
My little butterfly keeps me well fed
Why should I mutter?

)Moondog)

Now is the time for all good women to come to the aid of the
other women.

(Cynthia Nelson)

I tremble sometimes when I remember what that quilt knows about
me.

(Marguerite Ickis, quoting her great-grandmother)

But sleep
can only give us the pleasure of pleasure

if we're awake.

(Lyn Hejinian, *Redo)*

Alone

Is blue sky still as vibrant
with children's voices
the pull of something nameless
to occupy
with many names
my time.   I have
no words
for the air to make objects
ring.   I am finally alone.

Every object in this room
takes up space, having texture.
The chair so silent
and angled standing
reflected, shadowed not straining
one part against another.

Alone, I
have been searching
for you
who is no one
else,
not even an I.

So many things to do
in the world
all with a clean face in the morning
when sounds and light are most
together.   Can you bear the stillness?
Repeat it until it becomes exciting
like a jewel

a vibrating thing with no sound

Alpha Beta Catalogue

There is a cool space
where my childhood sits
vibrating and ready

it is not exactly heaven
it is not even kitty heaven

it is white and spacious with rectangular walls
Attended by a man with a reverence for toys
He polishes the card catalogue to a burnished ash

By myself
I look up "witch," "cat" and "magic" to find both
black and white

My dollhouse beams in on the counter
The tin hotel lights come on and flash red
To the Stegosaurus under Saturn while
Above me floats another undiscovered planet

Ballad of Amiri B. (60's)

Once was a man
    Name of LeRoi Jones
To be a culture worker
    In his bones

Down into the South
    Drove the coastline
Said this country
    Ain't no way all mine

Charleston was a sauna
    No sign of breeze
Even though he prayed
    Couldn't even breathe

Went to Ol' Miss
    To look on Faulkner's grave
Said *Ash to Ash man*
    Look who's the slave

Old man he said
    Better look see
Your most intimate photo
    Is history

Baraka: Blessed Amiri
    Only stayed with his
Signifying strongly
    All the unfinished biz

Wouldn't talk to white boys
    Larry F. and Allen G.
Even though used to keep
    Company

But Larry told the tale
    As the subway flashed by
Amiri gave us whiteboys
    A wink of his eye

Ballad of New Orleans

for Robert Hayden

Georgia May Frances
    Egyptian eyes
My momma was french and
    My daddy told lies

Said I was just like her
    Leading mens on
Pulled out a picture
    Of her man done gone

In the poor house with the jaundice
    Died the other week
Still feel his spirit
    Hovering over me

Got too much fluid
    Doctor pump it out
Makes you over-sexed, girls
    Now you watch out!

Young man he walk over
    Bunny painted on his leg
What about it, Georgia May?
    As she pat his head

What should I do girls?
    What should I do?
This young man's got a conjure—
    We're going to the moon!

Ballad of Vertical Integration

for Harry Golden, author & civil rights worker

Civil Rights was brewing in a Charlotte coffee shop,
At an orange juice bar called Tanner's
   down near the main bus stop.
Cross of Trade & Tryon where the Cherokee once hunt,
Harry Golden cast his shining eye on a way to make his point.

In a country of strangers from either side of town,
There were only certain places everybody could sit down.
Here black & white—both alike—stood UP and drank their juice.
"Eureka" Harry Golden cried "That's the way to call the truce!"

Take out all the CHAIRS from restaurants, cars & schools
Get rid of all the benches—Make way for other rules.
If some folks can't sit down somewhere then everybody STAND
We'll learn & eat VERTICAL—INTEGRATION in this land!

He printed up his paper—*The Carolina Israelite.*
Only in America he then went on to write.
Gold dust shines in red clay—We pass on from the past.
Harry, thanks for tickling our funny bones to help the changes last.

Now it's year 2003—just look around you how
Things aren't quite as far along as they ought to be somehow.
This ballad is a call to arms to open up our eyes:
Each and every one of us, Golden can arise.

For each and every one of us, a rainbow is the prize.

Car Games

for Beth

My head flopped on her lap in the seat as if dead
She yelled for a cop
"Dead Head, Dead Head
Gorgi's poor tender Head!"
Disembodied, from the front, to stop the "fight,"
our mother's hand made
circles in the night.

We made up a very dangerous trap
to fill ourselves with pleasurable dread.
The cars behind ours never would stop
stealing little children to use for their bread.
"Gray Car, Gray Car" we said
with a gasp, as the headlights
hit us through the back seat in red—
vampire cars circling the night.

Our third game after an engine lull nap
was to call Spirit World and see what they said
about us and our future and when it would stop.
Our faces projected as if from the dead
onto rear window, the stars for a shade—
an illusion on glass with aid of the light
of cars passing and passing away,
circling the night.

We made a cave, a fast-moving bed
in between all the gangsters and spirits and light—
Didn't matter where, what direction we sped
as we lived in our little circle of night.

Catullus Couch

for Bill Berkson

Good advice: "Start Over"
Today I am Catullus
fitful on my couch

Yearning for a playmate
to "write erotic playthings"
with
back & forth
as we promised . . .

Never missing dinner
Waking from Southern Living

Cows chiastically low and moan
non-chiastically arranged

O how lucky a poet is
who has only to feed her
self a suggestion or two

and later find it spilled
recumbant
into poems small enough
to carry
anywhere

Falling asleep with the small
green anthology in hand
I read through day-closed lids
illumined

Change this, Lesbia,
(meaning the verses)

Even then our love
remains.

Dear Rod Moth

for Rod Smith

You are a moth hitting me in my chest of film.   You are the brother of my southern wonts rented out to Madison Square garden for a Dead fest.   You are the Last Jupiter Baedecker. You are an Ornamental Flower Sculpture who smokes packs of feral wolf cub tickets outside the DMV.   You are one of the few people I feel is genuinely interested in trading off licks of colored icing like an Abstract Expessionist Rasta.   You are Barbara Guest on Mercury Rev.   You are Father of Pookie.   You are F stop on my knee and the subtitler of Rose Pizza.   You are my garden in the dark.   You are washing down a Klondike fuzzbuster with the Soft Drink of the Carolinas.   You are Burning and Adjusted, you are suffering the little children to come to you in the morning but you are not Jesus.   You are dancing that way to make people look down.   You are losing it with Kevin Davies. You are keeper of Buber.   You are a Bob Mould song structure bridging to the Emperor of Ice Cream.   You are here. You are 1000 characters in a spliced Passion slash Noh slash Morality play.   You are Aunty Diluvian's spire.   You are the alphabetic browser of Nebraskan glass.   You are scotch tape to be continued.

ESMERELDA SUITE

Euripedes' "hideout" cave is believed to have been found,
identified by a clay cup with his name on it.—New York Times

Coronary Decades to Crown Heights

Five days later
  We're still having fun
Cracking open the bow ties
  Of the chefs of metropolis
Eating whole plateaus
  Mirrored in your eyes
White reflective jackets

Pouncing escalators
  of MOMA's undulating
Frank stairwells
  Chrome cigar gardens
lit by C notes
  modern seers
pluck the electric cacti
of fur coats
in line
thanks for the
jump start
cut up
nervous taxi
my heart: Frank *is the better part of*
your heart poetry?

Red dot on my forehead:

married to poetry
more like a neglected lover
Or one I save up for—
Express the F stop—I'm reading to Queens
your poetry beside Anne Bradstreet's
to my dear and loving husband
which Harry Diaz read and
remembered
2 lines of
so I'll bring the whole thing
to him to class
to read and
enjoy tomorrow

The Current Scene Continued Which I Love to See

The world's not safe for Poetry
We must cordon off the Zones

For even relaxed, sprawling Spring
      so akin to me

Gasped for breath
     to watch
film's poetry

Unwind beside me, you
I too love to see

On bed or in
montage flicker

red   velvet   arm   rest

you take off
your daily mediating lenses

(which I also love to see you operating in)
     or reflecting
     movie flicker

     I wonder

who wrote
potent as were your kisses, enter here?

not Melpomene

who's skewered
or better
yet
dispersed

Desire Device

"My body's back and there's gonna be trouble"
(Jeff Derksen)

O buttercup
Desire is the ground
from which to act

A vibration setup
that must be registered
        that
I walk into
        notice her
hair clean & mounted
    up in modern shell

then I see another's
    streaked w/
later
realize
she's my old lover
I didn't even recognize from behind

& she's trembling slightly, her hair

        with coffee or what?

We're older
Her hands are still smooth

The ground from which to
        act is Desire

yet that's a hard
     path—
Its ground shifts

Time goes on

We're still
  here
    it takes courage
      to face, to fact it
without dread

Yet another one
reads poems
    that have good rhythm
    to write to

in
black smooth leather
her hair is longer
    since last I saw her

Esmerelda Suite

This is the bed . . .

Based in Esmerelda

I forgo the triple bipac
    tracked

to radiating spheres

of which I sing.

The single solitary singer

is not—

is not tuned into

one frequency only.

Tough jelly on the "El"

Skipping out to Hookerbocker

for the daily bread run

Looks like she's

ready to jump

to the good music

for once

to transcribe those bags

of drossy stuff

into

higher powered powder silky

What were those
    boys I was to

    transform?

Almost remember

    Please do

Character recognition now

(Something about

    transforming

everyday ?   (life)

  into

    poetry (?!)

The potentials of junky spring in a black notebook

Love lies sleeping under the grass

    bed still green

        purple tangle

      green vetch

    city garden

The garden gone to seed

      tumultuous

Bird voices
      hinge on the air

  What's picked to grow

    wild

Is other than where

      I'm from

Sign says

Holding area———→

point on a vector

    coughing

Red sorrel

  draped in

pine

  bough cut

to keep the purple arcs in

  brambles
 winter

garden
    locked

lights on

    tousled

    Beds

Poison of Gold's Fly-by-Night Signatures

Now come the Naysayers

Some people feel

Sick for beauty

and detraining

to & fro

with
Kitchen Scissors

Convulsive Beauty
&
Steady Beauty
wrote an Etiquette How-To

Inventing a new kind
of sugar (not judged)

It just dissolves on
the solvent edge
of a prompted vector

lifted up to a
better method
of making steel studs
in a gridded minute
of weekly error control

Wonderful substitutes

deflect the thrown
rocks of perpetual danger—

Our Lady of Associational Thinking

In this land of analytic

prickly anybody, we
skipped to New Sunday's
reckoned feminine delights:
Edible Gold
disneyed up to
a fly-by shooting.

Hannah's Method

Hot
As
Not
Now
Asking
How

When
Everyone
Is
Near,
Each
Raining

How Glad

Amazing sentences from Mother's Letters

For the time being, the doll is in the freezer but that will not solve the problem forever. When I got the house all decorated with dogwood branches which I had forced plus camellias and put the Ukrainian eggs you gave me on my popcorn dogwood branches, we were all ready for company. If you are acquainted with any nutritional "health nuts" who have some new suggestions, please send them. I served slaw & Herlocker's Barbecue heated in the special sauce which Bob had gotten on Highway 29. At one point he turned several summer salts on the floor while he continued to play the instrument which is curved in shape. This past week I went to the Black Forest Book Store where I asked the owner to help me find a book that would be especially good for Esther Massey Prince's grandchildren (when their mother dies of a brain tumor) which may be soon. We were amazed to see that the children's choir was made up of nine Hmong children plus 6 American blondes. Whoever has the most pennies in the jar has to kiss a cow (perhaps a calf) on December 10th. She told him that she was going to Washington to see the Dutch artist's exhibit with "someone else." I cooked thin lean porkchops.

Joe Acrostics

Just
Over   Bunches of
Easy   Rain
        And
        Indigo
        Noises,
        Androgynous
        Roses
        Do it again

+

Jinxy Beautiful Features, an Alphabet
Oracular
Ebony to

Bring risky fixtures to my
Reading, my
Alternator brow, a go in-between, an
Inner uninterrupted error or
Night sodden blue velvet
Apt to break over
Rare gray fealty in
Discs of what permission slips

Open Sez Me (T&G)

Rabbet is a groove or cut made in the edge
of a board in such a way (thrust back) that a
'nother piece may be fit into it to form a joint.

Wet edge of a rabbetted board, otherwise
engaged to the other,
set down your paying work &
tongue & groove
me again, an autonomous
arbitrix of institutional
negligeé, lost yet again in the dictionary.

Procrastination Sonnet

Be my lesbian cover band while I
again rest and negotiate the ever so scarlet
sparse dream notations as the year
turns red or orange not yet to mark
the students' papers that way since
it's like they did something irreparable.
Sheer exhaustion from what?

Maybe I should learn to write
about unpleasant daily world
more or else I'll have nothing
to say

Quantum Sonnet

The particle waves—in your firmament—comb
A golden mane—thereof—a graph—

Cruel behavior's handiwork— undone—
All phenomenon O Lord—can laugh

At the bright apparatus—of redeemers—come
To circuit round sharp amplitude—

Jumpstarted—wavelength—honeycomb
My commandment—to your frequency's mood

Thy experiment is way past way—
Outer space—Meditation's intensities

Convert play's determing eye—
To sight—jolt my light propensities—

To click my arms around your glory—
Converting gentler light—to photon's stranger story

Short Talk on Revenants

after Anne Carson

Zombies walk the hills waiting for a ballad to jump out of their eyes. Pay attention to what song is going through your head. It means something for your life. Change your tune—Change your fate.

The Sleep That Changed Everything

Private cheek pressed in pillow
book damp and red tender tether
Typewriter up and working
Snow is falling on New York

Greenwich Avenue & Jane
"Burritos" hot pink
Only me and my mind
Snow is falling on the Avenue

On top of the telephone booth
three flights down
drunk on salt fish
rich cream

Snow is falling under the lamp
In Nick's sync sound film
West Village quietly filling
with snow from the window

of his apartment somewhere
near here years ago
You were traveling in
South America writing
200 page books of poetry

I've been reading the travel section
at 29 years old
Some people come here
for vacation
I feel right at home

without many earthly possessions
to clutter my action

As in travel or dying
A full cab glides down Jane
to flashing yellow lights
It's still snowing

On New York

Two Ways to Rule

One with a big fat pawprint stamped in the middle of the illegal
pad nothing to do with interlocking narrators telling the stories
of non-existent films. Words all around us which wave sticky lit-
tle hands for our attentions or a four-square fragment ballad on
the wall not typed in yet. I dreamed the dream of forgetting to
go home on a six o'clock flight after hugging someone new sur-
feit of desire but no anchor—then we detoured for direction and
got caught up in further horror of looking at a woman who felt
no one looked at her so was out for revenge on innocent us.

Why is there no period at the end of sleep?
Does that make this illegible to some
Do I futher complicate matters
trying to be convolute
Or letting my convolution rule, growing out of control?

It's "Art."
If I say it simply will I lose your readers' attention?
(Of complex constuctions of the rolling seasons)

Movies enter poems so easily
then slip back out again, another fact of life.
She (B) & I have written spring but what about Fall.

I'm supposed to move into *less reflective territory?*
Everything turns into autobiography
Or else try to figure out how to write
Again so I can do it again
If all goes well I think two pens are open
        (simplicities are glittering)

but CAUGHT at
that old question
to be direct or obfuscated
If purposefully, then no good?
Maybe it's indulgent
to trace mind's multiple movings.

The How & Why Wonder Book of Trees
            was to be my
                        her
Golden Book of Words
which she changed to
The Secret Asexual Book of Kitten Words
        just for me

She said I had a "language problem"
but I am just trying to let gorgeous risk in.

I had and have lost lots of secret writing
I say after her saying "Don't you want some?"
I didn't publishize everything.
Now it's lost including some really good sex description

My will was not strong
        enough to change the word.

Everyone I know
        will die—
Another one did yesterday
The energetic Dad of a
        beautiful new friend

I spoke to mine on the phone—
when will he be satisfied or ever happy

with himself or me
Or is it others who won't
Let him be?
From whence in our family
this gloss of pressure
Desperate to be good
enough
I fall into leisure
until the last enormous
possible moment
to post mark

Vibratory Ode

Collage to the rescue . . .

*I need a book to say "I love you," the distance of another's words to
say what touches me most. Or is it that it needs to remain masked?*

(Rosmarie Waldrop)

*Discontinuity in my experience
to me means radical coverage. With garrulous*
                              [scanning

(Lyn Hejinian)

Vibrata bears down on a bow of air   ❦ 67 ❧

A Brownian Motion

Defines and goes

Psychedelic

Remarks on Color

Not mauve remarks on color

The weeds of Queens

Redraw the forms of estivation

Many years ago Spring came here:
/ /

In her color theory class, C was concerned with the
political implications behind:

> *white comes forward*
> *black recedes*

> *The colored man is asked quietly to resign.*

> (W. E. B. Du Bois)

In next seat
such lovely men
discuss marriage and ring fights

check this out
I told him
check out what she does
where she goes
everything
before you dedicate all your time
check it out

> *you're right man*
> *she stiffed me*

let's talk about something else
let's talk about cars

you're kidding me man
no I'm looking for one
going uphill downhill
doing 120
but what I paid for it

"So, why do birds make you so squeamish?"

you remember when the Seville went to that tapered end?
I didn't like that
        (refurbished two-toned seats)

After All, Regan Manages to Return   ❦ 69 ❧

                        (Washington Post)

(to write a regan renga)

Vibration of a song

mixed

strange Easter

mourning doves

bright blue

dark blue

yellow with black dots

fuschia

mauve Marlene diaphonous dress
structured up under her   cross-her-heart

with "Mopar" Meyers

Today's Easter Dog Fashion show:

the winner was dressed as Jesus
in robe   tied with a rope dragging a cross

One day years ago Spring came in

Bands named Make-up   Cosmic Vulva   Violent Anal Death
Tequila Mockingbird   and Pig Havoc

(I'll write *my* 437 East 12th Street)

Allen Ginsberg (left out the women) stood on
a stepstool four feet from his front window to photograph the
mass of people with silver balloons coming out of Mary Help of
Christians Easter Sunday 1995. Out front is a table of Ente-
mann's cakes, a man leaning against the wall of the funeral home
reading a tract surrounded by that curvy bouncelight that hap-
pens in cities off windows that makes me think of Bernadette's
lines from the sonnet "Holding the Thought of Love"

Of the subways and at their stations is today defused
As if by the scattering of light rays in a photograph
Of the softened reflection of a truck in a bakery window

not that the lines *describe* what I'm talking about
but are sort of *next to* those windows which generate
that amazing luminous light that exists only in cities
and are hard to quote without quoting the whole poem
because of her gorgeous

> *And to render harmless a bomb of the like*
> *Of such a pouring in different directions of love*
> *Love scattered not concentrated love talked about,*
> *So let's not talk of love the diffuseness of which*
> *Round our heads (that oriole's song) like on the platforms*

of Beryl, Garnet, Jewel, and Gem

Diamond, Opal Figments within

watch the turn of yonder screw

We sacked the city, Feverfew

Underneath it all

the colors are unbraiding

Underneath it all

Wittgenstein often lectured in English by producing bursts of a few sentences that were bracketed by tortured silences.

(Tractatus = brackets)

Practice Preface

I'm wanting to be affected

interpenetrable desire to justify

my fight for

speaking in bursts (femme language)

I / I

I write sometimes in a lower calmer voice

It's about really listening to

When I listen to myself

I hear the world

In Cut velvet versions

The full spectrum song cycle

Cycles of desire, cento songs are

Wet airs on tweaked vellum

Sustaining the vibration

We did the colors over the phone

My cento memories are   Your interventionist centos

a speech colors

the end of my dream I saw

2 child-size typewriters:

Olivetti
        like Anne's

and

a new one:

        Linguistica

Today I read

fin de siecle go-betweens and alembic trips

the flower forms of raworth/heavy light

        and literal Hollo flowers of Anselm

slide around in the book when I try to locate them again

I am not a product I

sleep on the bus next to stranger girls

half asleep I drift in pictures of flowered sailors

being cruel in turn and liking it

hear the voice in my own head as I travel

being no where or rather everywhere at once

it gives me that illusion at once to sing

and be sung, not committed to a locale

I yearn towards a longer form

THE VOLUPTUARY LION POEMS OF SPRING

for Matteo Ames

My Uncruel April, My Totally Equal Unforetold April Unfolded

Added cups and plates
        rotate other stars
                in your sequential platforms.

As with all good (real) poetry movements we splice the past
Aprils, walking near himself before there, her pleated heart,
                    heated.

The Question Undoes Itself on an organic twittering machine
Trumpet vine of the Bottle Brush Fire
Escape playing itself on the grassy beds

Of Hyacinth, light-bulbed, headboarded, made up,
Observed, vibratory-color bannered sheets of
Fire Sabi beauty, old peeling, jumbled, a mess.

The purple Third Avenue L, the Horrors of Spring.

Ecstatically crying, to peaceful well-being
Maintenance of the handful of unhatched speckled
Eggs thrown from the next nest, mixed with
The hand-drawn line so far from your usual practice.

The Impulse to Call & Spring Upon

As incremental desire is counted out
So I kiss closer and closely to your mouth
The No Blame Chaos Form complete

A surge protects our hearts from sleep
To see you closely, across from me, I'm
rising, decisive, almost shy

Your eyes, lionine—my poetry
Risks gushing kisses so I close my song,
Anticipating our playing alone

        I didn't know how

this little

       song would

end

the last stanza not right

until last night

  when

to change the form

to Leonine

everything

    like the form

  is changed

a long long line

  like your sweet kisses

which liquefy

my limbs

  & get better & better

          impossibly

           real

❦ 77 ❧

Complex

I came into Matteo's Aims
I came into Matteo's Zones
This finding of Fact of
This Binding effect
Yes I feel familiar
  to you yet don't know
        you at all
yet totally look forward
to getting to know the
        Specifics
        geological
We both make special
piles of paper in
our attempts to organize
and shuffle reality
Do definitions change reality?
Are your eyes always
  that color?
Do you know my eyes were
green the morning yours
        were blue

Ma Lab

We are able to move
We are able to sew well
Wet tea roars on storms
Rome Born meets lost teams alone

Amo
Amas
Amat

Women or Men, we are
Well
We are sore sonnets
Lambs roar
More wet
No More Alone
Loss Sewn
Eat lore's stews,
Morn, moan nor roam

Voluptuary Lion Poem

I kiss you one Septillion times
My (lobo) Serval deerlike (wolfen) lamb
And on the Septillionth kiss I will start
again to unfold the bath of my tongue upon you
Blue sepia Indri, equidistant
from Malagasy *indry!* look! (mistakenly assumed by the
French naturalist Pierre Sonnerat to be the animal's name)
a large lemur having short fur and a silky tail —
Indo-Iranian court song to You, my golden love
whose body glows in the bath of my ivory-mirrored mind's eyes.

Menage a deux

a mix of the world, here
of all the works in
         our possible realms
a foretelling   then
a worry   you say don't
the world has its wears
         and its surprises
both sublime and nasty
I feel a strange peace
         in your arms

from which action
         could happen
         seasonal

Think of how you
         felt as a human
ten years ago
   Who was around you?
   What did you think important?
Here's to that rough
architectural magic, that strange
   presence, exhausted,
then tumultuous, on fire,
   never predicted, yet
eating breakfast slowly
going to work, breathing
off the ferry a little cat
runs across the approaching
dock in the warm breeze
as we bump into the new pilings

I remember my grandmother's
White Ford Galaxy
  covered
   with
  loads of pink
  petals like wet
   Kleenex
    damp
    heavy
   damp
I have a darkness
I'm afraid to divulge
Name it, bring it into the
  light—will you still love me?
I want so much to open
that I'm afraid I might crack
  —afraid I might freeze

May Visitation

Again at the foot of our first bed
Now dark blood-purple tulips
   have thrust up strong
near Star of Bethlehem
Red Columbine
and all around
         purple iris
wish you were here
fragrant & dark
all the leaves bursting
willow & your wisteria
rose leaves mint   to list
the flowers isn't it
enough?

You Are Not Gorgeous and I Am
Coming Anyway

You are gorgeous and I am not getting to know you any better
I feel Broken into I feel drench dreamed
With the Woolworth's worth of dimestore socks
Photographed and networked up a racoon's nest
Not here in the city but in the ill de la cité

Hungry for some foreign country
In the middle of my jury duty crawl
Into bed exhumed from Björk's Champagne toast
To all of Iceland's fairy cultures recorded
As the doors swing open and shut

Of course you are gorgeous and I & I am coming
It happens every day and then I fall into the crick again
Spattered with immediate boredom
Feeding two boys not one and neither of them hitting home

Transposed to his trappist ringers
Nick called this morning from Assisi,
Last words as the phone card ran out
Blinking from 600 lire down

See you in the next life

DEVASTATION

an overwhelming

or

a de-vasting

stuck

All is loneliness here for me
Loneliness here for me
Loneliness
　　　　　(Moondog)

　　　　　Abide with me　　Fast falls the Even Tide

　　　　　　　　　　　　　(as played by Monk)

　　　　　I left a Funeral, in my Brain

　　　　　(typo in index of *Oxford Poetry in English*, 1987)

　　　　　When tenderness is detached from the source of
　　　　　tenderness, its logical outcome is terror.
　　　　　　　　　　　　(Flannery O'Connor)

　　　　　Pain always produces logic, which is very bad for you.

　　　　　　　　　　　　　(Frank O'Hara)

Animal Planet

Those who can

Do

Those who can't

Fuck

Those who can

Ballad of Phoebe Steele

My husband, Ed was a very fine man—
    Went off to school in the East.
He did depart for the land in the West
    For to turn our famine to feast.

He staked a claim upon the land—
    Stretched forty by forty wide.
He then returned to fetch me and the Babes—
    For to be right by his side.

His arms and heart were as fine as steel—
    On him I did rely.
'Til the typhoid came and broke him down
    I was far too numb to cry.

Scarce eleven day in our new homeland—
    My Babes and I were left alone.
The marriage tree where our door would be—
    Stood straight though his soul had flown.

I rolled my sleeves and I set to work—
    Plowed the fields all on my own.
Under prairie sky, fiery dawn to dusk—
    Straight rows I made from stone.

People of the Earth, keep silent watch—
    Give me aid when you can
People of the Hills, up above the range—
    Throw down much-needed rain.

Now I lie still, down in my grave—

In a different spot from my unmarked man.
My children's hold is fast away—
  They no longer own the land.

Though broken down the land's still there—
  Many a year we did our part.
She provided us with a meal and a prayer—
  And a stone shaped like a heart.

Ballad of Susan Smith

A Modern "Cruel Mother Ballad"

I put my car into reverse
On a lee and lonely
This will be my Babies' hearse
Down by the green lake side-ee-o

I am a daughter of the Mill
On a lee and lonely
Young I am but doomed to kill
Down by the green lake side-ee-o

I had a love I thought was true
On a lee and lonely
The more he rubbed the redder I grew
Down by the green lake side-ee-o

Left high and dry and all alone
On a lee and lonely
These Babes weigh me down like a stone
Down by the green lake side-ee-o

I see a dark man in my dream
On a lee and lonely
He'll be the one to take the blame
Down by the green lake side-ee-o

O No! O No! What have I done?
On a lee and lonely
To please a man I've killed my sons
Down by the green lake side-ee-o

Naught will cleanse me of this sin
On a lee and lonely
To please myself I'd do it again
Down by the green lake side-ee-o

A Nation's pity for my plight
On a lee and lonely
I look so innocent and white
Down by the green lake side-ee-o

Black Man, Black Man, I accuse you
On a lee and lonely
On Nationwide you'll get your due
Down by the green lake side-ee-o

How can a woman rout her womb
On a lee and lonely
But not close her babies' tomb?
Down by the green lake side-ee-o

My face it cracks at what I say
On a lee and lonely
I'll spend my life in prison gray
Far *from the green lake side-ee-o*

"You did as much as dash our brains"
On a lee and lonely
"Blood on your hands is our refrain"
Down by the green lake side-ee-o

My Babes! They speak—The cold black lake
On a lee and lonely
Shoots forth its hand, more souls to take
Down by the green lake side-ee-o

Bitchin' Blues

She done laid her little body
Beneaf my breast,
And I won't never
Git no rest.

　　　　　　　　(Sterling A. Browne, "Conjured")

Been this other woman, taken over my rent.
Now there's been this racy woman, taken over my rent.
Thought she was just there for living,
But it's in bed that she's spent.

My baby's going to get it, if I ever see her face.
Baby's gonna catch it, if she ever dare show face.
She's gone and plowed me under
And I can't stand the pace.

Her and her music, spiritual and fine . . .
She says she needs her writing, fine　fine　fine
But the way that she's been acting
Seems she won't find the time.

Jewel, you know I love you, and we have to be apart.
Girl, you said, "I love you, but we're gonna be apart . . ."
But you must know　how this just stabs me through the
heart.

Break

in Case

Of Grammar

When she's dead
the best thing about her
won't be that she loved that man

but I do give her credit
for having done so

Her baseball words   Terrible
Her sea lyrics, vast   93
as Spicer hisself
as a grammarian blues & melts

icy hot this vehicle
has been checked for
    sleeping children

Bridge Over Troubled Daughters

Poet's body still young

racked with pain & grammar

I have fallen through

   the rabbit hole

of whole lives already

aching from all the

births I've given

broken up longing

swollen with blood, unmarried

one more ride through town

with flowers in my hair

in Euphrosyne's car   rebuilt

looking for my mother or grandmother or

start to show and lose everything

or do it alone, past desire

Campion Cento

after Steven's score

Author of light

Break now my heart

Our pleasure sleeps

This place I remember

Control of the Music

So much on your plate

No love in vain

But then I dwell on it

Things change

It's come after me, you

Then "THAT'S ALL FOLKS!"

    The best emotional mess of me space

                      now

Had to open up again

    Handling instructions

Some people never do

    Where it touches itself

Embarrassed by human tears

Still here at a playful distance

the death of love is
very different from the
death of death

I.

strong Italian coffee
   cushioned
chairs wrought iron
how random our loves
seem on location
baby's breath &
hearts on a string
or string of hearts
we sheer our lusts
away now for the
winter
the sap contains new desire
beneath—strong clear
swelling liquid peacefully
expanding do not flee
the garden there is
much to bloom yet
the bats & birds of
your innermost thoughts
are arriving from Fiesole

Leave the quiet & they
will find you even in
the talking streets
   invisible hinges around
your centoculated shoulders
alight & then not

the cut nerve in my
neck tingles back
to waking the deep
bruises rise to the surface
of the skin to bloom out
dissipating into humid
air he mutilated
the garden for me
now the rose dies on
a pillow in a darkened
room

2.

I've been here before
a familiar death's never
expected vines a small
spiral she checks the
progress of the drying
clothes, so old *there*
will be another but will
it always come to this
loss of excitement
the dog crashing through
the garden after a
bird

3.

I see

the mist of

Fellini

a white sky

My gifts never

received

not taken

so really never

given

how

unhappiness

changed

my body

O for the

drugs of love

to numb

constant

thoughts

Deep Gossip

The whole shifts   the world that is
written specifically   every remembered
for the chain   sequel

elegantly pursued

something called   or not deep gossip
"   " is lost   no separation my
or just misplaced   fixity italicized

I can't sleep

to splice   moving or doing it
or be that way   slowly be clear
is my question   an able architecture

our nonexistent wedding

still writing   finds a terse
"is it happening" or   love still too
it is happening   abstract isn't it

but won't play or   forgetting how to
shut Death away   deep gossip not

ERASERS

for Louise Bourgeois

I don't want
To be erased
By someone else
I tell myself
I can go on
I tell myself
Some others choose
To erase a line
Or many lines
Everything is so geological
of mine
How can I write
The next spidery book
Knowing it may be lost
Next year
or tomorrow
I take a bath
and sleep some more
I wake up and remember
again the words I lost
It's all up in your mind
my father said
I thought he meant I was being crazy
but I guess he was being kind
But also saying It doesn't matter
If you lost your notebooks
You can write them again
Which I Can Not
Because I am
An other

Than I was—
Same childhood
but with—new fissures
or filters
more layers
that won't wash
away with
black soap.

fragment
ballad

(O Death)

loved one's

  loved ones

we laughed

  goodbye

  generous

  all we can do is

  hold them

like I held

  wanted to be

do not desert

  us life not yet

we have to hold the other

on to us the living

    let go

For Strength

Shells of stone
around my home

The lost things
are lost

Like ice slow lightning

I will not please
you anymore

Now
Am I ready

For the miracle of my life

Fully Emily

for Marjorie Keller, sister condenser

Valerian Emily

Fully filmic Emily

Full of

Cake

Twin cakes eaten so sweet
Sisters too much
Sisters not enough

Where is she?
Where is Mar Mommy?

The cats unusually at opposite ends of the house

We are stardust
We are golden

Space so black like the bottom of the sea where the flashlight's
  beam is lost.
You cannot see the stars while they're forming—they don't
  give off any light yet.

Maybe she was here to take me to lunch.

She is still here giving off a light.
She is here in the Lemon Poppy Seed Cake she brought me last
  week still in my freezer.

She told me that she was up at 4 or 5 in the morning to do her work and an old woman came to her door with a suitcase. In Vermont the ice & snow were everywhere. Margie took the woman in off the porch to the kitchen. She asked the woman, "Who are you?" The woman looked confused and scared and said, "I don't know." "Where do you live?" "I don't know." M. made some calls, found out who she was. M. relayed the look of relief and recognition on the woman's face when her son arrived. I now exclaim: How fortunate it was that she came to Margie's house!

> The cake was a gift
> passing through such a generous presence

Regret! Regret!
Never knowing
Never getting to know her better!

> I admire the way she is so open
> the way her voice is steady
> Open, kind to everyone

How do we tell you now we love her now?

I heard Zoey say
"maybe she was here to take me to lunch"

> maybe she was

Fully Emily

in

the human realm

in

human memory

he helped me saying

> When a friend has died
> I've felt the sense of the place they were
> That place sometimes is where they were stuck
> In that place how people are
>> helping them commune with that place leave

> how
> leave that place
> helping them leave that place

> be with them
> be with them
> tremendous know
> buddhist car
> burn a photo of that person
> it sounds odd
> space isn't that
> cold medicines
> the darkest thing
> instructive

> falsity will be taken into death
> subtle artifice
> in order to survive
> little lies actually hellish
> embarrassing
> luminous melon
> negative

claustrophobic
push through it

Kodachrome green
Framing on

I love standing in the sunlight with my Bolex

I've learned how not to make the birds flutter

I've learned how to become invisible

.

Garnet Degrees

Disgorged palm trees

drink Tia Juana leather

juice cross tiger lily frets

of set tequila gradients

Slap all out—your name here

tweaked & tender again

adopt-a-wreck

enter wrong way

Happy to walk the tracks

just like a telecaster

in her own little burb

she faxes so lightly

Ground Base Marked Personal

to Steven Taylor

> *"The child!*
> *The child is not automatic!"*
> (Carla Harryman, *Vice*)

Call me up when you want to make the child

Otherwise I'll be in Oakland
where there's no there there

Or in S.F. smelling the bougainvillea &
        dodging bull's blood roses, orange

I'm trying to glimpse the animals in the zoo
Any help you can give me will be much appreciated
The bus schedule is such
that I might miss dinner

The desires to be everywhere

I can afford you

A great degree of freedom

You can be professional in the sun

If only our regular slow metronomic ground
swells can emanate out and hit back like a wave

Half-Heartedly

My Dictionary of Stitches

Does the Maple Leaf Rage

Institutional Velvet

cold halls   begotten / relish
                    whether

What faults he had
(For who from faults is free?)

blight with plague this marriage hearse

no tolerance for alcohol

      suppose to be

Actual Honey

Planet Saturn turns
    baby rick rack
so fetching against a tourniquet bib

It hurts so quirky
Patchwork mind out on a limb

as bland as pink woolen footies

No   Matter   What
Only Touch the Front

Art impoverished

  a starving lullaby

Hello little baby
I am the Mother

Kleptomania's Darts

a dart is

something particular to one's own taste
a quick movement
a tuck   in a dress

kleptomania's darts

are in my

Quitted Quilts

my blue corn necklace
gone in a past daycamp
temporarily knows my way home

movement
        children
            love
        random

Condensed time signatures

Left-over cento

Dexter

Ambi

out of Left Field

Cento:

   Lines
from all my Books   before they are

                away

Now all I have is nerve

A book of titles

I wanted to have a child while I was still young

so I guess I'll have to stay

       younger longer

filling the blanks
holding an orange
I learn not to feel
more numbly subtly
schitzed out on reception
painful heat still arises
mystified I go on

I shall appear in a complete dress
of purple   with a list
of the beauties I have conquered
embroidered round my calves

I could go on this way

an appearance of poetry

forms

referents shifting

Who are "they?"

(I feel that often in a way they link)

Sick & exhausted

in major world cities

burned by salt

mismatched gloves

deciding what next

these are the same ears that

ache in the wind

in weather & people

I was released

in separate rehabs

as "final solution"

translation of physical form

to Portable Altar

Quilt with objects

sewn on

Guilt Quilt

beautiful absences

of the present beau

Memory is gone

zaps onto voto nub

do not blanket

comfort snow

unmet family

unknown future

possibilities eat

a sugar gap

Milagro   Hand   Infinite

don't mix up   not ridiculous

within & under language forms

extricated weather

such a focus

wonder if we'll still

Mural

I've already written

about the space between the o and e

in poet or should I say

of it, with it,

prepositions being

any way a squirrel can jump

The Aleph-Bet contains my sister's name

    to the tune of Barbara Allen:

In Charlotte-town where she was born
there lived a fine young fiddler—
She's open to the winds of change
Around her glows the filter

of lightning bugs around the clock
and hoot owls in the distance
Why can't they see nor feel nor touch
Her fiery well-honed pistons?

Out West, pioneers buy TVs

to drown out incessant winds

which once drove them mad.

Thank God I live near Chinatown

where I can get a fresh supply

Of Power Beauty Girl Stationery

mean
while

Selena is shot in her hotel room

in Texas—dark blue comes

up through the dove window

ruffled   covers up

respite from love's scaly talons

hiding in my bed with

the generate grammar

my aching hanky

what else reverbed?

Death's

Disbelief and the

ephemeral touch of

word on You

Political Funeral in Black & White, What Can I Do?

I was walking way East on Houston
the other gray day
and saw wheatpasted flyers
for Matthew Shepard's
Political Funeral
on the silver phone poles and
they were starting to peel off in the wind
and I thought I should take a picture
of them for this poem
but when I came back they were
gone or covered by others

What can I do about this now?
Nothing to photograph, to prove
they were there

There were pictures in the paper
of people arrested,
shoved on NYC buses
at Matthew Shepard's Political Funeral
attended by many many more people
than anyone expected
What can I do about this now?

I can think of him
I can write this poem
Etched into all our skins are the descriptions we read—
of his body and what they did to it
Once read they may be covered
but they remain etched into us our skins

We are changed and must change
We must other our lives
How how how could this happen
We all know how it happened
Even though we want to deny it's still like this
We know this could happen again

Someone by accident or design put a sign
over Essex Street and now it's Sex Street

We all live on the Sex Street one way or another so

Let Everyone Build and Live in the House of their Own Lovely
Desiring Design on Sex Street Openly If We Are To Remain
Human We Must Love the Visit of Neighbors like us or Unlike
No One is the Same When will People Stop This Killing off of
Feeling Unspeakable Remember Again

A Single Bard

for Allen Ginsberg

Sing, Singer!
Grain a bell
I see he bade a line

Sing, Roar!
Beguile a grab bag!
Rub bare!
Grease a ring!
A Raga burr!

Eagle beginners arise

A Niagara Rage
Rinses, Singes

+

Always
Loving
Life
Even
Now

Alive
Lips
Laughing
Every
Night

Great
In his
Neighborhood
Songs, to
Brooklyn College,
Every
Ride
Going on

+

Everyone is right now playing their own Allen home movie
in their mind's eye.

Sleep Talk

Half asleep & talking to myself
Boys bang cans outside
Many letters to write
It sounds like rain now

Boys bang cans outside
Masculine, Feminine
It sounds like rain now
As cars drive past

Masculine, Feminine
Clothes hang on the wall
As cars drive past
I rub my own neck

Clothes hang on the wall
I prepare my own dream
I rub my own neck
I lay out the cards

I prepare my own dream
Many letters to write
I lay out the cards
Half asleep & talking to myself

So Inside

My gown's inside out
It doesn't matter
Sea glass music still
Breathing the air

It doesn't matter
My hair is uneven
Breathing the air
Outside where it's colder

My hair is uneven
My blankets are thick
Outside where it's colder
You will wake up

My blankets are thick
I let you alone
You will wake up
I feel better

I let you alone
Sea glass music still
I feel better
My gown's inside out

Solar Loss

Not all babies make it
should the blossoms touch

Sonnet Around Stephanie

What rituals are in Benares?
Our little cat's grave smells of incense, earth—
three candles, three days now, burning.
Through the window from my desk I can see

them in the dark. Beneath yellow leaves
is the earth we all pressed down, turning
it over to smell it dark with ferns.
His spirit plays in shadow, we still see

it in the halls. In my mind, your self-portrait
slowly unwraps suicidal arms to show your face.
Blessed are the small, for they shall be buried.

Blown into darkness, I could only wait
for the Gift to come around again—drawn to empty space.
Blessed are the angry, for they shall be carried.

Villanelle on Being Alone

Helix adored falls open to sick heat
This has everything to do with you
I will not think of when next we meet

Do you have enough to eat?
Which voice will I listen to?
Helix adored falls open to sick heat

I'm linked to you, Others—Speak!
But need to be alone—in situ
I will not think of when next we meet

Night's humid compass repeats—
Cantilevered desire comes to
Helix adored falls open to sick heat

Another minor tragedy—my problem—boundary
Bee sting / lightning storm—new
I will not think of when next we meet

The cramps pursue their mother ship. Finally
the blue fixed voices appear to you
Helix adored falls open to sick heat
I will not think of when next we meet

Villanelle to Beth

Sister O Sister O Sister I said
We still have a pact on the coming of age
Hear the heartbeat, the wild child is not dead

On daisy-fried eggs and rose petals we fed
We swore to be free of the growing up cage
Sister O Sister O Sister I said

When I was your age he loved me to bed
I stopped playing Witch, your eyes filled with rage
Hear the heartbeat, the wild child is not dead

I sleep alone now, just books in my bed
I feel your first lover soon on the stage
Sister O Sister O Sister I said

Go dance your life now, circling black, circling red
But write in both colors on the first page:
Hear the heartbeat, the wild child is not dead

We'll meet later on, the wild child in our head
Old mountain women of red clay and sage
Sister O Sister O Sister I said
Hear the heartbeat, the wild child is not dead.

INFLORESCENCE

to begin to bloom

❦ ❦ ❦

a flower cluster or sometimes a solitary flower

❦ ❦ ❦

the budding and unfolding of blossoms

But defeat will be made into rapture.

(Carla Harryman)

The fire you like so much in me
is the mark of someone adamantly free

(Liz Phair)

To turn, turn
Will be our delight
Til by turning turning
We come round right

(Shaker hymn)

I have broken loves
Though they've never me
Turning once more—
Large cat is gone
Look again   petal open

(Coby Batty)

& was actually sorry

     when it was
     completed

    very little stability in my life

     I remember feeling very satisfied
   at the completion
  of each quilted flower

a known cellist
hand-stitched this piece using scraps from her concert gown
mostly silk

while camping we saw a meteor shower from our sleeping bags
& this inspired the background fabric . . . she had shiny black hair
a love for anything unusual & a weakness for bright green

She has seldom gone long
without having a needle & thread in her hand since that time

In Infloresence

for
Agnes Lee Dunlop Wiley
who is
Obaa

Some people aren't long
for this world

What can I do?
Not leave them alone til
then that's for sure

O
Be
Alright
Always!

On
Bed
Asking
Assurance

Oak
Bending
Ages
Already

New Orleans Airport

Rose's Yellow Taxi

Service Anywhere

A.K.A Transportation

I stood here before

in the shimmer-heat

with you now it's cool

2 blossoms face in opposite directions

A boy—white paint splashed on jeans
falls through the multidimensional Pollock

It hasn't fully hit me yet

Her faint voice

The lowest she's been

I'll see her soon

Blue Streak Cab

written in lightning bolts

Front Porch — Gene's House, 'Moss Hotel' in view

Camellias in a row

Fully transformed into a Zulu rider,
Blake Antoine feels the formidable
heft of a pair of painted Zulu coconuts

        is a newsworthy item here
        in the *Times Picayune*

A bird song I never heard before

A man in red flannel plaid pajamas
walks between the camellias
and the water

My poems are in The World
in colored ink—bright pink
with illustrations—in my own
hand right in the middle
so they are the first you see
in my dream

I live with Julie again
on the opposite side of Ludlow
Hill—Uli is angry with
Flavia and we have 2 tanks
of amphibious creatures

A New Orleans man was found shot in
the head in a burning car Thursday
morning in Gentilly.

I choose to live here, not in fear.

The way I remember it

My third thought upon waking

Everything is in fragments

Lying within hand's reach

Ready to be assembled or not

How can I return to the black hole
        or deep blue lake
        of 'beautiful' grief—so cold it hurts

Not always up to speed—my body needs

Restorative Sleep

I hope you get what you want

Obaa said to me as I hurried
        away, having missed my adult
        plane, having fallen asleep
        beside her again

You know more about writing in one minute
than I do in A YEAR.

I still want to go deep with somebody

Death & Editorials

It hasn't hit me yet

Transformative Sleep

Destabilizing sleep, transitional

Think about how you would want to go

A Shadow Anywhere

I'm thinking about how

I want to go

to heaven

I see a shadow

Anywhere

Ruby the Human Figure

"You know you're from New Orleans
when everything else looks like Kansas"

Cry Cry Cry

Predestination dance of the senses, polyglotted onto 'Some Greek Girls.' Are you planning a song subterraneous? Fellow teachers—prop your legs up and repeat after me: I will open my cards to the flow of the waters of *Mel*-po-mene Pumping Station, read all 80 books for Cynthia's best and learned the logos of fabric hearts. Help me, Help my unbelief. Respect your elderberries and tune into their repetitive birdsongs—feed your ancestral costumes and imagine how to how to. The filmic strings that hang around my neck can lace into red Jacob's Ladders or Sawmill transitory to Witch's Hat or Tarzan's Underwear.

However did you get her up?

She's slipping away.   I want so

for her to hold

my baby   her great-granddaughter

(I wrote a letter

to anticipated daughter-to-be
in junior high school orange notebook)

Now *she's* a baby to her daughter

My mother, Dora Lee

Beth said Mom must be suffering

Through this alone—no brother

to help her

Purple ribbons for

                              Justice

Yellow (gold) for Power

Green (Faith)

As to the beads

Throw til it hurts

The Midnight Novelist in All of Us

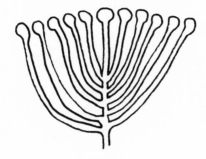

Corymb

Lyre-like

silver lodge of sound

of music the muse's din

the corymb is a plectral

graph—I want a dulcimer

to play with a feather—

I want a bowed, stringed

thing like a Kinari

or Kelvinated rake with

strings plucked & sung

tongued and booked to the

water's edge that breaks them back again

instruments of praise

bagpipe   (squeezed and fingered simultaneously)
concertina
Autoharp
dulcimer
Kora
Mbira
fiddle
Lyre

what was that instrument
the woman upstairs
said could be bowed & plucked
at the same time?

Psaltry

Obaa I Remember

I loved when we went to

visit you at Covenant Church

You took us to the big kitchen

where the woman was baking biscuits—

fresh out of the industrial oven—

hot butter & grape jelly!

One morning staying with you

I remember you woke us up

very early—One side of the house

was pitch black—the other had

Orange sun beams through the trees

I was very excited because we

were going to the Library!

I remember first holding Beth

sitting cross-legged on your kitchen floor

so I wouldn't drop her

It was Halloween—I

was Three!

I wore the yellow duck mask

& a raincoat for my costume.

I remember spinning around and around in the wingback chair
that sifted out "graph-ite" on the rug.

I remember your den's knotty pine paneling
faces grinning out through the grain.

Where Alchemical Sentences
Stitched Alphabetical Pain
       Through the sampler of someone else
                Plus Obaa
                Plus me

Measuring the progress of the illness

Will she die before the end of the alphabet

No she is strong

Small quick cycles of pain & rest

working from right to left or from any direction

writing from deep within the world of the family

Starting a new color
with a long length of thread

Her eyes are so sad

Circadian narcotic

Equals sleep

Interstitial

Incremental

Spent the last hour on the out of the flower

Writing little by little

cross & back
as it occurs

How close I am to the dream state

now days

Am I having all of hers?

The needle point of stitchery

Intravenous field

Red Velvet Cake

Sally Lunn

chinaberry
laburnum

elaegnus

ligustrum

gaillardia

linaria

galax

pyracantha

Housing the Human Eyes

Obaa has turned inward
'snoring' with eyes open
kissing the napkin
Not seeing us—
Is it up or down
or the last time she focused

I was exhausted,
ran away from home
for one night
Is it ever the same?

Never

What does she see?
I know she feels

Title far away from the poem

The last thing she said to me
at this point is 'more'
When I fed her grits
       raspberry yogurt
       raspberry applesauce

When will her journey end?

She said 'thank you' too—
    many times

February 14

                                        early am

Stitches gone wrong
I keep taking it out

The wrong number of stitches

Beth's push & pull

140 heart rate

per minute Obaa

1 year ago 48

90 / 60 = Blood Pressure

Temperature 100.1

I withdrew, no where to go

Still here

48 breaths per minute

written in her book she'll no longer

write in

I am uneconomical

Can't sleep, drop stitches

When I touch her I feel things

Deciding not to leave until, no

you first no   you

short dips & curves

We're right here
We're not leaving

what is the prayer I should say?

Once (before)

I sneezed, and said "Bless You"
(speaking for her as I thought she wouldn't speak)
She said "I *hope* I can bless you."

All these flowers

do they take up the oxygen?

So many camellias

being killed by the frost

I asked Obaa
        (when was that, Monday?)
Who I should make a valentine for—
She said "Me"

The bamboo sheets look like bones—

Beth & I went into the woods & found many sunken graves

What trays can bring us anything?

Why

Are we born to die?
To lay this body down?

Let me continue to be generous

Not close down

Be Present Here

    & Now

with Obaa   & my mother & my sister

I knew something had changed when
Mom let the bathroom light be out

Obaa Agnes Inflorescence

I Love You   are your words
I Love You   are mine

The continuation your own
Of your mother and daughter.
You live in the details of my words and my actions.

You are with me no matter where I go.

You are the flower of my matriarchal line.

You are the flavor of Sally Lunn.

You are the generous sunshine
In the basement of Covenant Presbyterian
Where we came to visit across
Softly shining waxy tiles—

At the cool wooden desk I sat on your lap.
You taught me to draw a three-dimensional square
And how to sing

> *Stintilight, Stintilight!*
> *O globular Vivific!*
> *Fain may I fathom*
> *Thy nature's specific!*

> *Loftily poised*
> *On either capacious—*
> *Greatly resembles*
> *A gem carbonacious!*

When I asked "Is that in *English?*"
You started me on my lifelong love of language
To the tune of *Twinkle Twinkle Little Star.*

You say "Lee Ann really *likes* New York. Well, she can *have* it!"

The last words you say to me are "more" and "thank you"

Theola holds me and reminds me of you smiling.

Beth draws the beautiful arc of your nose over and over.

Mom sings *Long Ago* many times.

I sing *Come go with me out to the Field*

And

Let down thy Bars O Death takes on new meaning when I lower the bars
on the side of your bed.

Breathing more and more slowly,
We watch you change and go.

It feels like fine gold powder everywhere, diffusing.
After a hard time, you are leaving slowly and gently.

You are ready to go.

Beth sees you in her mind's eye
Above a whirling pool of gold
Being greeted by Van, Dudley, Dodo and others.

I lay my body down in your bed after they take yours away.
I can see the birds in the window, the sun coming up,
Pictures of Beth, Janie, Mac and me on the wall.
Camellias on the dresser around more photos,
A little cardboard house.

You are in Inflorescence even now.

Let us be the flower of our matriarchal lines.

Inflorescence   to begin to bloom

Inflorescence   to pass through fire

Inflorescence   to bloom after passing through fire

Fine gold powder is shining, peacefully changed.

(the good bye)

your absence makes a space for me to be
thinking you are still there like a moth
dusting me with listening from a distant
distance. I can say a good bye without fear
And when you return my dear which you
seem to do the buzz continues its
modulatory measure pleasurable
alternately unpredictable as all alive things are

My epithalamion

a bird sound at the end of every sentence
the period dissolves and becomes a curve of notes

from *lake of souls (reading notes*

(Robin Blaser)

on the morning of my would be wedding
I wake up and turn again to poetry
halfway cross the continental drift
towards a blazing island
I open the Holy Forest
to middle epithalamion
and later tell Robin the story
of how maybe now
I am married to poetry
and he says But don't let *him* go
and I don't for a little bit longer
but now everything is changed and not
so bad as I bed down with poetry and myself
whom I each love entwined real love and would welcome another

Red Fox

Red Fox jump into my path
   Shining there in the sun
Then he gave me a little laugh
   Flipped his tail & run

Blackbird drinking in the watergrass
   Twinkle in his eye
Feathers shine all purple-green
   Then away he fly

     Shady Grove, my little love
     Shady Grove I'm calling
     Shady Grove, my little love
     You're the one I'm telling

Chickadee rustling in the grass
   Spider on my thumb
Dragonfly is on my knee
   I am not alone

Chipmunk hanging from a straw
   Baby as he could be
Then he showed me his little eye
   And his soft belly

Looking for the One I Love
   Could that One be You?
Looking for the One I Love
   One who'll Love me True

Shady Grove, my little love
Shady Grove I say
Shady Grove, my little love
I'll be back some day

Do not touch the Columbine
Leave it there in the Sun
It'll fade right in your hand
See what you have done

Sustain Petal

Come on, you who remembers your dreams
Who acts upon them in this world
Come you who I often and silently call
so that I may be with you
Come and sustain me
and I will sustain you
with what sustenance I have
with the curls of revolutionary quiet
with lovely baroque convolutions of thought
Come make with me a baby
of both of us
A new and separate being
with brothers & sisters
born & unborn
Who we will meet and recognize
as time progresses
we know not
How
Yet
isn't that the
Beauty of it
late into the nights
early in the Day
sleeping and waking
when apart not separate
for the distant vibrational hum
if I listen under the earth
lets me listen to myself
The Full Register
of the Earth
and

all Musics of the Spheres
the waters
we have within each other
and all around
the very air
Share our perceptions
Respect our quiets
Heal our hurts
throats and necks
backs and hearts
Protect to Open
Make a new life
For those around us fully
and for those
To come

To come
To

The Words of Love

I thank the world it will anoint me
If I show it how I hold it

(Will Oldham)

I pledge allegiance to the lamb
And also to the other one
The march is long and now I stand
Again on ground fresh broken

    I had small difficulty made
      In keeping up with your parade
        The underbrush was heavy, dense
    With sounds of distant fire

    I've been cut & I've been frayed
      Then spliced as whole as any maid
        Despite this rending I have stayed
    In aisles of trees amongst the shades

    Our loved ones they have gone
      Far from camps of death and harm
        We're still in this mortal coil
    Words of Love as leaves unfurl

    Now you & me we're each alone
      Yellow cake & marrow bone
        All sense of fear now pass away
    I trace a map along the way

I pledge allegiance to the lamb
And also to the other one
The march is long and now I stand
Again on ground fresh broken

3 Rings

Once I had a garnet ring
                    garnet ring
                    garnet ring
Set in a thin gold band garnet ring

My father gave it me
But it was not to be

For I broke it with a twig underneath
                              underneath
I broke it with a twig underneath

Then my mother gave to me
                          gave to me
                          gave to me
A silver dogwood ring
                          from a tree

It has petals four
I'll wear forevermore
On my right hand
for all to see

The love I thought was true
                          Ne'er gave me
                          Ne'er gave me
A ring of earth nor sea
          Earth nor sea

Instead he gave to me
Three things I cannot see
And they ring inside of me
                    O my Soul
                    O my Soul
They Sing inside of me
                    O my Soul

Vision Crown

for James Yamada & Lisa Smith

I sing this Crown of Hymns
    Twined in two leafy wreaths
Come o'er the sea
    Cross boundary
Sung in these Blue Mountains

Inlaid with rarest gems
    This garland now will weave
All manner of inspiring fire
    'Tween Heaven and Earthly Love

Crown them with Fiery Crowns
    As Double Helix turns
The vortex of
This Wondrous Love
    Forever more will burn

Abundance of our Love
    We gather here today
The ever-widening fiery Spheres
    Together let us say:

Crown them with many Crowns
    A Crown is like a Ring
That circles round us all in turn
    And sings and sings and sings:

Be Thou My Vision
O Love of my Heart
Naught be all else to me
Save that thou Art

My own true Love
By day or by Night
Waking or Sleeping
Thy Vision my Light

SOME SLEEP NOTES

Insufflation

p. 4 "A Call for Vertical Integration in the Eye of the Storm": Note by way of Explanation from the *Double Southern Register* or is it *The Southern Lyre?*

Who is burning these churches? Make them stop!

After weaving our way through the new upscale Charlotte city-limit suburban scrawl out Rae Road through her country memory, my mom and I persuade the cop protecting the vacated scene to let us past the yellow and black plastic ribbons to see the smoldered mess, not much left—blackened beams, jambs kicked out by anonymous torch, red clay wet from last night's useless hoses—a little house with vacant front porch right across the street—I imagine the fear and go home and write this poem.

In *The Mind of the South*, W. J. Cash wrote that he and his generation "hated [the South] with the exasperated hate of a lover who cannot persuade the object of his affections to his desire."

Charlotte,

I love you deeply. That's why I had to leave.

I see your changes keyed up rapidly flashing past the new contra dance named the Independence Boulevard which is way convoluted like the traffic which is nothing compared to here, up North from whence I sign this letter,

Letter Out, Letter Back

p. 15 "Respond to me": Compare:

Responde mihi

Responde mihi : quantas habeo
iniquitates et peccata, scelera mea
et delicta ostende mihi.

Cur faciem tuam abscondis,
et arbitraris me inimicum tuum?

Contra folium, quod vento rapitur,

ostendis potentium tuam,
et stipulam siccum persequaris:

Scribis enim contra me amaritudines,
et consumere me, consumere vis peccatis:
dolescentiae meae.

Posuisti in nervo pedem meum,
et observasti omnes
semitas meas,
et vestigia pedum meorum, considerasti:

Qui quasi putredo consumendus sum, quasi
vestimentum, quod comeditur a tinea.

This is a Latin text set by Sébastien de Brossard (1655–1730) in a
musical program at Foundation Royaumont, in France where I was
in residence the summer of 1995 at the Atelier Cosmopolite. My ho-
mophonic mistranslation was originally published in *Miss Tradsuc-
tion,* a pamphlet I made, charting the experiments we did there.

p. 16 "shiny jewel eye"   "Single Girl, Single Girl, Goes where she
please. / Married Girl, Married Girl, Baby on her knees, Baby on
her knees" are two lines from the song, "Single Girl, Married Girl,"

sung by The Carter Family on Harry Smith's *Smithsonian Folkways Anthology of American Folk Music,* volume 3: SONGS, track 11.

p. 18 "Whitman Poem 'Come . . .'" parallels "Come Go with Me," my Emily Dickinson riff, and invitational, invocational opening poem of my first full-length book, *Polyverse.* Both poems were written on assignment from Keith Waldrop.

Estivation

Five of these poems were done in response to the shapes of the forms of estivation (dictionary drawings).

p. 22 "Involute"   The Lyn Hejinian quote is from page 70 of *Oxota.*

Vibratory Odes

p. 32 The epigraph is taken from this account from *Anonymous Was a Woman,* edited by Mira Bank (St. Martin's Press)

It took me more than twenty years, nearly twenty-five, I reckon, in the evenings after supper when the children were all put to bed. My whole life is in that quilt. It scares me sometimes when I look at it. All my joys and all my sorrows are stitched into those little pieces. When I was proud of the boys and when I was downright provoked and angry with them. When the girls annoyed me or when they gave me a warm feeling around my heart. And John, too. He was stitched into that quilt and all thirty years we were married. Sometimes I loved him and sometimes I sat there hating him as I pieced the patches together. So they are all in that quilt, my hopes and fears, my joys and sorrows, my loves and hates. I tremble sometimes when I remember what that quilt knows about me.

—Marguerite Ickis, quoting her great-grandmother

p. 33 "Alone" was written in Paris in 1985.

p. 34 "Alpha Beta Catalogue" was written for the store Alphaville, on West Houston Street across from the Film Forum, in New York City, which specializes in toys from the 50s –70s.

p. 35 "Ballad of Amiri B. (60's)," was written from a title given to me by Michael Harper at Brown in 1986.

p. 37 "Ballad of New Orleans" was set to music in 1999 at the Virginia Center for the Creative Arts by Tom Kimmel during a poet / songwriter collaboration session. It was also published as a broadside by Lit City, a New Orleans reading series.

p. 38 "Ballad of Vertical Integration" was composed to the tune of "In the Middle of Nowhere," by Steven Taylor and Kenward Elmslie, from their musical *Postcards on Parade*. Its subject is civil rights worker Harry Golden, who lived in my hometown of Charlotte, N.C. As the song says, he wrote an influential book, *Only in America*, and edited and distributed a civil rights newspaper, The *Carolina Israelite*, which contained his satirical essay on "Vertical Integration." His papers are housed at the University of North Carolina at Charlotte (UNCC).

p. 42 "Dear Rod Moth" The form is partially inspired by Bernadette Mayer's poem "sci fi lee ann," published in *The Bernadette Mayer Reader*, (New Directions).

p. 70 In "Vibratory Ode," "Holding the Thought of Love" is from *Sonnets* by Bernadette Mayer (Tender Buttons, 1989).

Devastation

p. 92 "The Ballad of Phoebe Steele" was a project in collaboration with Linda Kozloff-Turner, a photo/oral history of Centennial Farms around Boulder, Colorado, while we were both in residence at the Rocky Mountain Women's Institute. Set and sung to the Traditional Appalachian tune, "3 Babes."

p. 90 "Ballad of Susan Smith" was composed as a ballad to the tune of "There was a Lady Living Yore," or "There Was a Lady Living in York," collected at Mount Airy Fiddler's Convention, first weekend of June 1994, from Anne Doerner. It is a "Cruel Mother" Child Ballad. Thank you Julie Patton, for whom I wrote this poem, who had it on assignment from Don Byron. Thank you Harryette Mullen for writing this crucial stanza for "The Ballad of Susan Smith":

> A Nation's pity for my plight
> *On a lee and lonely*
> I look so innocent and white
> *Down by the green lake side-ee-o*

p. 92 "Bitchin' Blues" was composed in a workshop with Michael Harper and was the first poem I had ever set to a tune in collaboration with Steven Taylor, at the Naropa Institute during my first of many summers at the Jack Kerouac School of Disembodied Poetics, 1985.

p. 94 I want to thank Dee Dougherty and Shelley F Marlow for the phrase, "Bridge Over Troubled Daughters."

p. 96 In "Control of the Music," "THAT'S ALL FOLKS!" is a quote both from Looney Tunes, and from a drawing by Joe Brainard in the UCSD archives.

p. 100 In "Deep Gossip" the poem title is the last two words in Allen Ginsberg's "City Midnight Junk Strains, (For Frank O'Hara)."

Infloresence

p. 133 "& was actually sorry when it was completed . . ." The epigraphs are a patchwork cento of notes I wrote down from descriptions of women's quilting processes in a lobby display of the University of Colorado at Boulder library, circa 1996.

p. 134 "Obaa-san" is the honorific for "grandmother" in Japanese. I called her that because Agnes Lee Dunlop Wiley became my grandmother when I entered the world in Japan, October 11, 1963. Thank you to Matteo Ames for writing the third acrostic dedication for "In Infloresence" out loud, plus other words and ideas in this book.

p. 156 Thank you Julianne Swartz for asking me to write "(the good bye)," which inscribes a particular moment of parting, and for providing the cover art on the original cover drawing for the Tender Buttons pamphlet of *The Voluptuary Lion Poems of Spring.*

p. 158 "Red Fox" was composed to the traditional folk tune "Shady Grove" at Yaddo, then set to another tune by Pierce Pettis at the VCCA songwriters and poets collaboration, 1999.

p. 160 "Sustain Petal" is a cosmic want-ad written in summer 1999 at Yaddo.

p. 162 "Words of Love" was composed and sung to a variation of the tune "minor place," a song by bonnie 'prince' billy on the album *I see a darkness* at the Virginia Center for the Creative Arts.

p.164 "3 Rings" was composed to the c. 1811 American folk hymn tune WONDROUS LOVE or "What Wondrous Love is This?" at the Virginia Center for the Creative Arts.

p. 166 "Vision Crown," the epithalamion for Lisa Smith and James Yamada, was composed to two hymn tunes spliced together: "Crown Him with Many Crowns" (Diademata) and, "Be Thou My Vision," which is based on an ancient Irish ballad. The second tune is also known as SLANE in the Presbyterian hymnbooks.